T0137547

How to Hate Trump and Other Poems Polemical

David Ewbank

Order this book online at www.trafford.com
or email orders@trafford.com

Most Trafford titles are also available at major online book retailers.

Print information available on the last page.

ISBN: 978-1-6987-1560-5 (sc)
ISBN: 978-1-6987-1561-2 (e)

Library of Congress Control Number: 2023919499

Trafford rev. 10/10/2023

 www.trafford.com

North America & international
toll-free: 844-688-6899 (USA & Canada)
fax: 812 355 4082

Contents

How to Hate Trump

David Ewbank

An ethical conundrum that's provoked
Bewilderment and endless perturbation
Might be succinctly summarized this way:
How does one avoid the risks of righteous indignation?
A synonym for *indignation*'s *wrath*,
And wise men say that wrath's a deadly sin.
Is righteous wrath, therefore, an oxymoron—
A sly, sententious platitude that lets the devil in?
Waxing wrathful in a righteous cause—
That sounds a bit like saying that wrongdoing,
A devious means, is justified whenever
The end that's got your dander up is one that's worth pursuing.
And if we're honest, isn't it the case
That virtue can be tainted by a vice?
One can, e.g., be proud of one's humility,
Or snub a snob, or slight someone by being extra "nice."
That's bad, of course, but moralists are prone
To presuppose that life's less hard and vexing
Than actually it is. To tell the truth,
The choices that we have to make are cryptic and perplexing.
Condemn the sin, but save the hapless sinner.

That sounds alright—it's noble and august.
In practice, though, can one, say, chastise lying,
But for the liar feel no complementary disgust?
Books on ethics tend to be abstract;
In life one's always faced with concrete cases.
In treatises the good and the bad may be
Profound ideas. In life they're always folks with human faces.
Now, it's a fact that Jesus reprehended,
Wrath and rage and recommended love,
But even Jesus, perfect though he was,
Of giving vent to certain piques and peeves was not above.
Just recall how angrily he drove
The greedy money changers from the temple.
That was not a loving act, now was it?
Commandments and imperatives are sometimes just too simple.
I wonder: can we find a middle way
Twixt moral law and nitty-gritty fact,
And hate the bad *because* we love the good—
Exonerate the actor though we frown upon the act?
Or is it sometimes simply just the case
That sin from sinner can't be separated?
In certain instances the wedded two,
Like up and down or right and left, seem intimately mated.
But lofty generalities must fail
To carry force when not exemplified.
Truths merely theoretical and vague
Command our willing credence only when they are applied.
To be precise—is splitting act from actor
A taxing feat that would confound and stump
The skills of even mild, forbearing saints

In the case of two-faced, insurrectionary Donald Trump?

*　　*　　*　　*

Off hand I'd say the answer's clear: it's no.
But such alacrity is premature.
The subject of our inquiry is hating.
Before we take so dire a step we must be really sure.
Dear reader, first, it's requisite to know
Precisely what it is we're disesteeming.
With Trump that duty's easily discharged:
Cheating, treachery, lying, lechery, greed and treasonous scheming.
His troubles with the law are legendary.
His probity's been constantly contested,
And he's a record holder when it comes
To chalking up complaints from all the ladies he's molested.
The list of law suits, criminal and civil,
In which the plaintiffs charge that he's to blame
Is longer than a hulking giant's arm.
As defendant Trump's a champ. What a shameful claim to fame!
He's uttered more than thirty thousand lies.
(That's right. It's documented. Check it out.)
And when he's told the truth and contradicted,
He'll cry "Fake news," and like an injured martyr pine and pout.
Of all the heinous lies he's told, the big one,
The one he falsely labels "stop the steal,"
Tops the list. It contradicts and cancels
Truth itself and redefines the meaning of what's real.
Trump's definition of a fair election?
"One I've won." The law in Donaldland?
"What's so is simply what I say is so."

Reality and sanity are banished out of hand.
To put it mildly, Donald's grip on truth
Is famously infirm and insecure.
Corona virus? It'll fade away.
Climate change? The liberal conspiracy *du jour*.
Bigotry? Some Nazis are good people.
Senator McCain? The chump was captured.
Putin, Bolsonaro, Erdogan?
By every autocrat he's met the man has been enraptured?
Remember rival Carly Fiorina?
He dissed her looks. No man would ever choose her.
A patriot—a man who's died defending
Our free and democratic way of life? A sorry loser.
The world for Donald Trump's a huge arena
In which he gratifies his monstrous Ego;
His "friends" are grasping, sycophantic fawners.
"A worshipful bootlicking toady"—Trumpese for *amigo*.
And so, dear reader, as we analyze
The moral ambiguities of hating
On one thing we may set our minds at rest:
What we hate's an issue that requires no debating.

*   *   *   *

But before we leave our focus on the man
We must address an argument one could
Advance in Trump's defense: he's narcissistic.
Ergo: he can't act the way a decent person should.
That he's a narcissist there is no doubt.
The way that he was raised explains a lot.
But does this psychic tendency imply

That he's exonerated from behaving as he aught?
Let's see: he lies and cheats. Well, what of that?
His demon, like the devil, makes him do it,
And so the demon's got to take the rap.
That's the weaselly way a strict determinist would view it.
(*En passant*: the narcissist himself
Must scoff at this defense. It hurts his pride.
"You're not in charge." That thought's the very thing
An "I alone can fix it" stable genius can't abide.)
So: Trump is not a fault—he's off the hook
If character is fate and fate's unbeatable.
But free will versus fate's a vexed debate
That's tricky and intractable. It's certainly not tweetable.
Suffice it here to say: I can't resolve
A mystery that's puzzled seers for eons.
In a matter so abstruse and rechrché
Poets, unlike sage philosophers, are merely peons.
But I know this: the world at large can't wait
For theorists to solve the dense conundrum.
Parents, teachers, judges have to deal,
Right now, with vital wants and woes of the people who are under 'em,
And a truly social world can't be conceived
If everyone's a mere automaton,
If no one's ever either right or wrong,
And every human action's a fatality forgone.
Imagine that the world is one vast stage
And human acts are pure and simple puppetry;
Responsible behavior—virtue, vice,
Morality and good and bad—they all are vain and up a tree.
(Ironically, a fatalist's upset

When anyone his point of view rejects—
Just as though, quite inconsistently,
He thinks ideas can be autonomous, not mere effects.)

*   *   *   *

Just one more thought about the man himself
(In stating it I fear that I might lose you):
Consider: being Donald Trump's no fun.
(I'm serious. I don't suggest this merely to bemuse you.)
You must think "What! This canting cretin raving!
In Mar-a-Lago Trump lives like a prince.
He's rich. He famous—idolized and praised.
Wake up and smell the coffee, rhyming moralist. Speak sense!"
Hold on! Back off! Dear reader, be assured:
In terms of crowd appeal, prestige and pelf
I realize the man's a lucky bloke,
But think of this: what's living like when he's all by himself?
The world, I think, must be a lonely place
If all you live for's riches and acclaim.
Though, as they say, there is no *i* in *team*,
There is an *i* in *rich* and there's a sneaky *me* in *fame*.
A fellow has no friends; he's just got fans
When all he cares about is me, Me, ME.
True friendship presupposes true respect,
Earnestness, sincere concern and reciprocity.
A narcissist can't be a friend because
The only one he loves lives in his mirror.
Love's a "going out," a self-transcendence.
For Trump the self's his only love. No other could be dearer.
And so, instead of friends, he has reflections,

Eidolons that replicate and flatter
The image of himself he dotes upon.
Can you imagine anything more isolating—flatter?
Now reader, if you're thinking something like:
"In a world replete with suffering and pain,
Why should I waste my sympathy on Trump,
A man whose lack of sympathy is manifestly plain,
A man who brutally imprisons kids,
So that they never see their folks again,
A sadist who believes a copper should
Behave more roughly when he takes a malefactor in,
A thug who says it's perfectly OK
To force protestors out and beat 'em bloody,
A jerk who ridicules the speech impaired
And thinks a person who objects is a grouchy fuddy-duddy.
Why pity Trump when there are more deserving
Multitudes whose far more serious plight
Puts Donald's sad neurosis in the dust?
The man is isolated. Well, so what? It serves him right!"
Alright! You win! To sympathize with Trump's
Not only profitless, it's inessential.
Let the blighter stew in his loathsome juices,
And we'll resume our scrutiny of themes more consequential.

                    *   *   *   *

Judged purely as a record-breaking braggart,
Trump would surely top a list in Guinness.
If that were all, there'd be no cause to fret,
But Trump, alas, is more than just a sicko—he's a menace,
And that's because he fully typifies—

Embodies and incarnates, as it were—
A multitude of keen, like-minded fans,
And does so well, the line twixt man and mob begins to blur.
Now, as we did when we considered Trump,
We must, before we instigate our hating,
Be sure of what it is we disapprove.
We need to take out time for rational deliberating.
It's one thing, after all, to say "O.K,
Go ahead and hate a man; he's terrible."
It's quite another thing to classify
Entire groups of people as detestably unbearable.
Trumpeters (let's call Trump backers that)
Are all alike and also all diverse.
They all are Donald devotees, that true,
But some compared to others are much better, some much worse.
One set contains the bosses; one the base
(A very rough division, I confess);
The bosses are politicos and pols;
The base is proletariat, but only more or less.
The base is far more numerous, so let's
Begin our pointed questioning with them.
Are they victimized and taken in by Trump.
Or are they fully culpable and guilty, just like him?
If we're to hate perceptively, we must
Consider and resolve this touchy topic.
If Trumpeters are victims, that's a shame;
If not, the stance we must adopt is bleakly misanthropic.
Let's see if we can sympathetically
Conceive the world as Trump supporters must—
Enter, as it were, the *mise en scène*

That inflames in them such militant resentment and disgust.

*   *   *   *

"The way the world's supposed to be has been
Screwed up and jinxed by liberals and nuts.
To earn his pay a worker busts his ass,
But welfare bums are given checks for sitting on their butts.
And hordes of down-and-out, free-loading migrants,
Criminals and rapists, on the whole,
Come pouring through our nation's open borders
To get their share of state assistance on the public dole.
And half the time the kooks that run the country
Ignore the gripes and griefs of the majority—
The badgered, law-abiding, working stiffs—
To please some lazy, belly-achin', pity-me minority.
Some fucked-up flake who's fed up with his gender
Identifies as female and will claim
He has a right to use a woman's john,
Though when he pees it's clear as day he's nothin' like a dame.
Some liberated 'Miz' when she hears 'Miss'
Flares up and gets her knickers in a twist.
There's nothing wrong with 'Miss'; it's just polite,
But she thinks every gentleman's a cheeky chauvinist.
Some goofball pushing universal love
Thinks saying 'Merry Christmas' insults Jews
And Jains and Rastafarians and Wiccans—
Anyone at all who doesn't share a Christian's views.
A hornet's nest of just such wacky weirdoes,
Malcontents and cranks of every manner,
Are welcomed by left-leaning know-it-alls

And proudly march beneath their stuck-up, phony liberal banner.
Politicos in Washington D.C.
Love giving tons of foreign aid away
To any needy alien who asks—
Screw the *us* who pay the bills in our own US of A.
We put-upon Americans believe
Our government requires a basic redo.
Throw out the snooty liberal elite!
What we need's a man who thinks and talks the way that we do—
Some winner who is very, very good,
Who's great, incredible, fantastic—huge,
Some real good guy who bigly knows the score,
Not some pathetic, overrated, losing liberal stooge.
I'm mad as hell and sick of being gypped.
Comrades arise! We're not wimps, we're men!
Let's back a man who's got the loot—the clout
To thump these traitor liberals and make us great again."

*   *   *   *

Toward such a fan what line should we adopt?
Regale the chap with facts and argument?
Give it a try, but don't be woebegone
If reasoning falls flat against such zealous discontent.
Consider this: the guy may have a point.
It's true that income inequality
Has reached obscene proportions—also this:
The cost of living's outta sight—that's no hyperbole.
All that's quite true; however, you might hint
That turning to a privileged billionaire
For sympathy is vain. For plutocrats

Socialistic sharing is their favorite bugbear.

You might point out that rich men don't love workers.

Instead they venerate free enterprise,

A system that makes everybody happy—

Or would if only teed-off workers wouldn't unionize.

Of the mighty flood of tax relief for Croesus

A working man may finally get a nickel;

By the time the benefits get down to him,

Despite what tycoons tout, the flood is truly just a trickle.

In short, the stock Republican agenda

Assumes the rich are valuable job makers

While working men (exchangeable employees,

Always out for number one) are parasites and takers.

How then, one wonders, did it come about

That, baffling and peculiar though it is,

So many workers hero worship Trump

When, truth to tell, their interests are, as plain as day, not his?

*   *   *   *

To comprehend this curious paradox

Watch a Trump-run rally on TV.

Observe: as his supporters clap and cheer,

He talks about the things he hates almost exclusively.

His vision of the future is defined

By all the things he likes to pan and pillory.

His favorite talking points are blunt and few:

For instance, "Damn the liberal press!"—"Imprison Hillary."

Does Trump present a vision of the future

That honors but surpasses what is past,

That taps into a universal striving

For lofty goals that we may hope to realize at last?
Does he concede that betterment entails
A lucid recognition of what's wrong?
The answer's no. Instead he recommends
Stifling valid discontent to keep our nation strong.
America, according to our Donald,
Was once a land where everything was swell
Before the Democrats and other pinkos
Usurped our great Utopia, and now it's gone to hell.
What does it mean: "I'll make us great *again*"?
Is the genocide of Indians a feat
Deserving replication? Owning slaves—
Is that a way of life he really wants us to repeat?
For Trump, to recognize the less than perfect
Aspects of our checkered history
Amounts to treason, and our guiltless kids
Must be protected from exposure to such treachery.
Progress for Trump is really retrogression.
What is this past he wants us to embrace?
MAGA's code for "In the good old days
WASP's ruled and blacks and laborers and women knew their place."
Trump gratifies his backers with such cant.
They love to hear him speechify and rave.
It isn't reasoned discourse that they're after;
It's crude, insulting, pure and vicious venom that they crave.
The energy that sets the man in motion,
The potent lure he uses as his bait,
The *idée fixe* that captivates his base—
It isn't love or real concern; it's simply hate, hate, hate.
Trump's a flowing font of enmity,

And I'm afraid that Trumpeters are too.
They're violent and virulent and vile!
I simply loathe the lot of 'em, and wish them ill, don't you?

*   *   *   *

My God! Dear reader, see what I've just done?
I've let myself be swept away with hate!
And that's the very thing this poem's about—
Not saying to it "Come on in"—but giving it the gate.
Oh dear! I must apologize. You see
How bad it gets when one begins to cater
To animosity and indignation:
Illogically, immorally, one starts to hate the hater.
Trumpeters are haters, that's for sure.
But does one want to emulate one's foe?
If hate is clearly bad in Trumpeters,
Then isn't hating back a clear-cut wrong we must forgo?
On the other hand (in fact we just have two,
But when some complex topic's being mooted
Hands get multiplied, and more than two
Alternatives are usually put forward and disputed.)
One objection to the standard rule
That good ends never justify bad means
Might be that, for the most part, Trumpeters
Don't think such moral niceties are worth a hill of beans.
They hate quite unreservedly and thus
Exert upon the world enormous power,
While moralists, by nursing pangs and qualms,
Succeed in having no effect outside their ivory tower.
Now reader, I imagine that you too

Might well be tired of doubts and vacillations.
"Give Trump and his supporters hell! Enough
Of inconclusive subtleties and endless hesitations.
The jerks are out to scuttle free elections.
This is not the time for being meek.
No more wishy-washy navel gazing.
What we need's a rough and ready *Realpolitik.*
Rarefied deliberation's out!
We need to face the facts. Real men and women are
Never moved by subtle disputation.
We're engaged in warfare not an academic seminar.
The 'war' has not yet come to open strife.
Net yet. But ponder January six.
'Kill the Veep!' 'Destroy and rack and wreck!'
That was not an exercise of normal politics.
We're threatened by an existential danger,
And if we lose, democracy's the victim.
Fight the foe with any means we've got;
Indulge in moral scruples only after we have licked 'em."
Alright! You win again. We've got to fight!
Though violence is not our cup of tea,
Up against such low-down reprobates
Decency, fair play and tact are futile trumpery.

*　　*　　*　　*

So since we're taking off the gloves, take this:
The Trumpeters who really are the pits
Are evangelicals—they're Pharisees—
Dissembling whited sepulchers! (i.e. they're hypocrites)
They prate of Christian love and brotherhood

And act as though they're out to save, not hurt you,
But "fundamentally" (excuse the pun)
They're bent on gaining power in the guise of boosting virtue.
A man's religious faith, of course, is private.
It's strictly no one's business but his own,
But when he seeks to foist his faith on others
He willy-nilly steps into an open combat zone.
Our federal Constitution's crystal clear:
Church from state must be well separated.
Fervent evangelicals, however,
Contend that that first principle is vastly overrated.
They say America's a Christian nation
When actually we're more a potpourri,
A veritable stew of sects and creeds,
But that's a fact rejected by tendentious zealotry.
Forget the Constitution—they believe
That all one needs to know is in *The Bible*,
Which only they know how to read aright.
They're ranting would-be theocrats, obsessed and fiercely tribal.
Teaching evolution is a crime,
Abortion is a sin that must be banned,
Having fun's a dangerous indulgence
(Though sex is tolerated if it's missionary bland).
Now Trump is neither reverent nor pious;
In a photo op the brand-fixated clown
Holds the holy book. But does he read it?
No. It's just a logo that he's holding upside down.
Though Trump's as pure and saintly as my hat,
To please the evangelicals the lout
Pretends to share their ideology

Because politically they wield extraordinary clout.
Now you would think to hear the stinkers talk
They're good as gold and holier-than thou,
But if you judge them by the man they choose
To represent the point of view—the man they worship. Wow!
All it takes to prove beyond a doubt
Their pious talk's mere glossolalic jabber
Is this: the standard bearer of their cause
Is a self-confessed, salacious, unrepentant pussy grabber.

*   *   *   *

Dear reader, please recall how I divided
Trumpeters into two different sets:
The base we've just examined; now the bosses—
The much more reprehensible of the two malignant threats.
How so? Because whatever can be said
To mitigate the malice of the base
(They're misinformed, misled, confused and so on)
Does not apply to men who know that Trump is a disgrace,
But who support the upstart nonetheless
Because the demagogue has such a way
With the *hoi polloi*—with getting them to vote
Against their vital interests and leading them astray.
(Of course there are a few politicos
Whose sponsorship of Trump is from the heart.
To call them hypocrites would be unjust.
Cynical they may not be; they're just not very smart.)
"Populist Republican"—what's this!
The combination sounds bizarre and queer.
In ordinary times, the different terms

Conservative and *leveler* would simply not cohere.
But the times are turbulent and out of joint.
We're in a fix that's quite unprecedented:
When Dives goes to bed with Lazarus
Republican, the word, is not what once it represented.
To *conservative*, its standard acceptation,
They've added *rebel, rioter, fanatic.*
Under Donald's leadership it means,
Not lowercase *republican*, but rather a*utocratic.*
A predicament as aberrant as this
Requires a helpful word of explanation.
I'll make it brief. The full elucidation
Is torturous and would require a lengthy presentation.
The task at hand is: damn those rotten bosses!
But a bit of background surely is admissible
And will, I'm hoping, help us understand,
Just why the two-faced fakes are so despicable and diss-able.

*   *   *   *

America's a democratic nation.
That statement's true, and yet it is a fact
Our founding fathers tampered with the franchise
So that that vital feature of democracy was stacked
In favor of a privileged upper class,
Gentlemen of probity and knowledge.
And so: poll taxes, property restrictions,
And worst of all that "check" on real results—the electoral college.
Some progress has been made (though not enough)
Toward making our elections truly fair,
But over time one constant's never changed:

Republican support of private sector *laissez-faire.*
Self-government is not innately wedded
To an economic ideology—
To one and only one—but to this fact
A doctrinaire Republican would fiercely not agree.
For him the opposite of *democratic*
Is *socialistic.* Simple. End of story.
That politics and commerce should be one
Is a cause in which he's fond of quoting mottos trite and hoary.
"The lifeblood of our land is competition."
"Enterprising financiers are heroes."
"The profit motive makes our country great."
"The welfare state creates free-loading ne'er-do-wells and zeroes."
Adam Smith's the champion of their creed:
Let open competition have full sway
And automatically a hand invisible
Maintains a perfect compromise twixt price and workers' pay.
To guarantee the hand can do its thing
You've got to have a level playing field.
That is to say, the working man must have
Equal opportunity with the congenitally well-heeled.
But that's precisely what we never do have.
In actuality the privileged few,
Those with wealth and influence and pull,
Have undeserved advantages—just like you know who.
Smith's theories work out splendidly on paper;
In fact that famous hand's not really fair.
It doesn't justly spread a nation's wealth;
Instead the rich and privileged always get the lion's share.
This stark inequity has been acknowledged

By Democrats who've sought to remedy
The worst injustices of social class
Created by the lack of wealth and opportunity,
But there's no developed country in the world
That hasn't sponsored social legislation
More liberal and sensible than ours.
And why? The bosses always cry "Left-wing abomination!"
By and large, the wider world has seen
The need for sane, undoctrinaire corrections
To strictly unrestricted *laissez-faire,*
And steered the ship of state in more responsible directions.
The bosses loathe all this and venerate
The state of things pre-FDR's New Deal.
Retrograde standpatters, they believe
Returning to the good old days insures the common weal.
But bucking change is always vain and futile,
Nostalgia buffs are doomed to disappointment.
Let's take a look and see how change became
A pesky fly in the archconservative's time-honored ointment.

*   *   *   *

Not only has our world transmogrified,
The pace of change itself accelerates.
Because the planet's growing ever warmer,
Our overstressed environment's been put in dire straits.
For decades now the world's been on the brink
Of nuclear disaster truly global—
Not just the bomb, we're also under threat
Of lethal "accidents" like Three Mile Island and Chernoble.
Our weather doesn't act the way it once did.

Disastrous floods and droughts are now the rule.
The air we breathe is laden with pollutants.
Oil is scarce and fracking's dicey. Soon we'll have no fuel.
But why go on? Everyone's bombarded
With news about such crises every day.
I needn't ply you with a longer list
Of all the many ways in which our world has gone astray.
But people too have changed. For instance, women—
Just like a genie once outside his lamp,
They won't be reimprisoned in their kitchens
Or be confined in pigeonholes that suffocate and cramp.
More generally, our population's changed.
Statisticians state with great authority
That in the not too distant future WASPs
Will loose their old predominance and shrink to a minority.
Now, how do staid Republicans react
To challenges that change has brought about?
They double down on ageless axioms
The truth of which they hold to be beyond the slightest doubt.
To wit: abolish taxes on the rich
(Or if not that, reduce them to a pittance.)
Cut reckless welfare spending to the bone
And thus put paid to the national debt—a firm and final quittance.
Industry's the engine of prosperity,
Not a present threat to the environment,
Laws that curb its right to foul the air,
Are tyrannies that should be put in permanent retirement.
Be stingy when it comes to spending, but
Don't stint on funding for the military.
Charter schools are great; they save us money.

Of course, support for art's a cause that's worthy, but not very.

The right to own a gun is sacrosanct.

(And that means everyone, not just militias.)

For any purpose short of homicide

A shooter should be free to do exactly what he wishes.

Government's forever regulating

Our food, our cars, our health, our work, our leisure.

That government is best that governs least.

Resist! Such laws are nothing short of wanton search and seizure.

Legislating from the bench is wrong.

Our Constitution doesn't say a word

About abortion. Thus, when women claim

The right of free volition in the matter, they're absurd,

And magistrates who slyly stretch the law,

In the name of common-sense interpretation,

To cover something new and unforeseen

Are steering our republic straight to wreck and ruination.

Oh, right-wing do's and don't's are arch-Mosaic;

On bedrock, adamantine stone they're writ.

The question is: On ever-changing life

Can a petrified, uncompromising creed be made to fit?

* * * *

Now, having shown that resolute right-wingers

To a mossback, retrogressive creed are wedded,

We must, dear reader, face a startling fact:

Of late the party down with rabid radicals has bedded.

In one essential, all-important way

It isn't true to say they haven't changed.

Indeed, it would be nearer to the truth

To say they've changed so much that nowadays they're quite deranged!

The change of which they're fully *au courant*

Is alterations in demography;

I.e. the population of our land

Grows ever less amenable to their philosophy.

The ultra rich, traditionally their base,

Are just as flush and powerful as ever—

Even flusher. Still, they're so elite,

As voters do they have a big effect on outcomes? Never.

The middle class, a bastion of support,

Into the proletariat's been sinking

As income inequality's increased

And the earnings of the *la bourgeois* have steadily been shrinking.

Of course, the working class has always been

Largely Democratic, but today

Their numbers have substantially increased

As more and more it's hard to keep the hungry wolf at bay.

So also more and more the right has found

It difficult their bill of goods to sell.

They could, of course, amend their principles,

But that, for them, is tantamount to going straight to hell.

And so they say: "Well since the right to vote

Is hedged about with powerful protections

And can't be abrogated, still there's this:

Make sure our party always wins by rigging the elections.

Our government already gives an edge

To wealthy individuals, so let's

Improve our preexistent upper hand

By fiddling with the ballot box and hedging all our bets.

First, we must do all we can to keep

Democrats away from polling stations

And make the right to vote dependent on

Fulfillment of a host of pettifogging regulations.

(Make voter registration hard to manage.

Require photographs on all ID's.)

Eliminate the mail-in ballot—that

Demagogic plot for letting poor folks vote with ease!

They must, instead, be made to stand in lines

At poling places rare and hard to find.

Only certain folks should find it easy

To cast a vote—select and well-off citizens—our kind.

And voting must be strictly supervised

By Republican observers primed to snare

Underhanded, sly and shifty cheats.

(Of course we must deny the fact that fraud's extremely rare.)

And voter rolls must be severely purged

(Though should it prove that purges operate

Impartially against both parties, then

We'll drop our eagerness for keeping records up to date.)

And gerrymandering—our age-old trick

Of drawing lines on maps so cleverly

Minorities will actually prevail—

That's a noble plan of action—and should ever be.

The electoral college may be out-of-date,

But since it countervails the popular vote

We must defend it with our very lives—

A plan that foils the Democrats and really gets their goat.

And finally, of course we must resist

Any scheme for making sure that voting

Is truly representative and fair

(That last remark is *entre nous* and strictly not for quoting)."

*　　*　　*　　*

Pre-Trump these stratagems were put in place,
All anti-democratic in intent.
They've had a dolorous effect—and yet
Some Democratic victories they were powerless to prevent.
"Alas! What can we do? We're at wit's end!"
The GOP bewailed its disarray,
But then a brash outsider crashed the party.
To everyone's astonishment the bounder saved the day.
At first, they didn't like the guy at all.
A hoard of party stalwarts tried to beat him.
They changed their tune, however, when he proved
That none of his competitors were able to defeat him.
Crude, profane, and oafish though he was,
He broke all bounds and changed the party's fate.
He showed those hidebound sluggards what it took
To mesmerize the multitudes and win elections. Hate.
Hate, and also lying. That was key.
He got his hoodwinked fans to put no stake
In documented, well-supported facts.
Anything that contradicted him he labeled fake.
He broke all records pioneering ways
Of benefiting from chicanery.
Did erstwhile critics see the light of day,
Snap to, salute, and rush to do his bidding? Yessiree.
And that's the way the Lincoln's party fell
From once-secure and honorable heights
(Conscientious slave emancipators,

Sincere, committed advocates of basic human rights)
To the dismal depths they currently infest.
A sickening, abject and woeful loss!
Who more than any other should be blamed?
The power-hungry party hack. The appalling pol. The boss.

*   *   *   *

And now, compliant reader, if you please,
Into our long protracted *tête à tête*
I must intrude yet one more crucial thought
To which, if we're to be complete, we must give proper weight.
We've spoken now of Trump and Trumpeters.
That is to say, we've dealt with humankind,
But now we need to talk about *Trumpism*.
A thing that has existence only in the human mind.
An *ism* is, indeed, a mere abstraction.
You'll never see one walking down the street.
It's not a palpably embodied thing,
And yet it's real, not some half-baked philosopher's conceit.
And this relates directly to our chat
Because if we deal only with one guy—
Trump, and only Trump—and underplay
The role that context plays in his success, we simplify.
It's critically important to remember
When Donald's antics make us grieve and groan
He wouldn't be a threat without his base,
He really doesn't *make* them hate. They do that on their own.
And also, if it really were the case
That Donald Trump, the man alone, was all
We had to fuss and fret about, one might

Take consolation in the former chief commander's fall
And argue: "Now the jerk has been defeated,
The twice-impeached has-been is *très passé*.
Let him rant and rage in Mar-a-Lago,
The sad, deluded oaf is harmless. He's *so* yesterday."
Such idle talk would be mere wishful thinking.
How pleasant things would be if it were right,
But Trumpism is still alive and well;
Trump not only could return, he absolutely might.
But my point's this: even if he died,
Even if the man weren't in the picture,
His treachery would be as spry as ever,
Threatening our freedom and requiring sharp-eyed stricture.
And this in turn directly has to do
With hate. We *should* abominate Trumpism!
When it's inspired by gross iniquity
Hate is just and thus immune from moral criticism.
So what, to put it bluntly, am I saying?
Trumpism's hateful. We should hate it. So.
Hate's okay if what you're hating's hate;
So hate away and rest content you've picked a valid foe?

*   *   *   *

But no! I simply cannot recommend it!
I know, dear reader—you're exasperated:
"To undercut the final, bottom line
For which throughout your diatribe so patiently I've waited!
What, if anything, can you be thinking,
You wishy-washy, shilly-shally poet?
Clearly, plainly state your poem's point—

Assuming that it has one and that by some chance you know it!"
I sympathize, my friend. I really do.
I wish that moral choice were less baroque—
That I could cut through hard complexities
With one all-solving, all-resolving, simplifying stroke.
I can't, but since you want it, here's a truth,
Hems and haws and if's and but's I'll drop.
You may not like to hear it, but it's true:
Hate's a dreadful, dire and deadly booby trap. Full stop.
Once you start to hate, no matter how
Justified you deem your hate to be,
Hate corrodes and rots and putrefies.
If you're in any doubt about it, try it and you'll see.
Untamed hating has a nasty way
Of morphing into passionate obsession,
And once it does it leads to zealotry—
To unabated bigotry and ethical regression.
And then where are you? Just like Donald Trump
And all of his unsympathetic minions,
You're infected by the very thing you loathe,
You're spouting hate and parroting detestable opinions.
Since this is so you see why I can't state—
Short and simple—hating hate's "okay."
(Such a meager, weak and puerile word!
A word appropriate for kindergarteners at play!)
The grown-up world we live in's not a place
Where plights are put to rights by formulae—
By simply choosing good and shunning bad;
The ways through adult conflicts are obscure and hard to see.
I wish the world were less equivocal,

And choices were as clear as day and night,

But as it is they're dubious and dark:

The right is furthered by the wrong, and wrong may lead to right.

It's quite inane to say, "Hate's wrong. Don't do it!"

Hate's a passion, not a willed decision.

When moral creeds and strong emotions clash,

Reason's often impotent to ward off a collision.

You hate a thing because that thing is hateful.

You might as well say, if you stub your toe,

You *shouldn't* feel the pain you really do feel.

Protestations of this ilk are manifestly *faux*.

So what we've got's a thorny paradox:

The world is chock-a-bloc with hateful stuff

Which we're innately programmed to abhor

But shouldn't because hating's wrong. I tell you—life is tough!

But the world is what it is; there is no other.

We have no choice. We work with what we've got.

So what's the answer? How is one to hate?

No more delay and persiflage! I'll give it my best shot.

I'll say this: hate's bad. Try to avoid it.

At least that's short, and maybe even sweet.

But also this: what good is setting goals

That you and I, although we try, can actually never meet?

So—face it—sad to say—hate can be useful.

(Maybe more than useful—necessary?)

Hate can be a vile but vital weapon

When you're up against a no-holds-barred, malicious adversary.

So *use* your hate. Direct it into channels

That do some good. Constructively employ it.

Treat it like a grim but useful tool,

But don't like Trump and Trumpeters delight in and enjoy it.
Don't *need* your hatred. Don't let hate define you.
What kind of person do you want to be—
A self-enamored hater or a lover?
Strive to be, not anti-Trump, but pro-democracy.

*   *   *   *

Well there, for what it's worth, at last, it is!
Advice so imprecise perhaps it's hollow—
Or if not that, so challenging and stern
In real-life, daily practice it's impossible to follow.
Hate, but don't become a hater. Yikes!
Sometimes I wonder—can one really do it?
Indeed, on some occasions in the past
I've tried to take my own advice, and, truth to tell, I blew it.
Still, I'll stick by it. Charge me, if you wish,
With advocating silly, sky-high pie,
But don't give up before you even start.
Success is far from certain, but my final word is *try*.

Old Leo: A Fable

(Dedicated to an honorable Republican, should such a creature exist.)
David Ewbank

Old Leo was grizzled and long of tooth.
There was little he hadn't seen.
Though his vision was blurred, his gait infirm,
His mind was razor keen.
It wasn't just that over the years
The old lion had learned a lot;
More than that, because of his age,
He had what youth's not got.
He was, in a word, wise, but wisdom—
More often revered than displayed
By those who claim a share of it—
Once failed to come to his aid.
How that was—the sad events
That led to such a turn
I'll undertake to elucidate.
Harken, now, and learn!

*   *   *   *

Lions, both in lore and in fact,
Are kings of the forest realm.

Nature ordained and fitted them for
Their rightful place at the helm.
Lower, feebler creatures will ever
Dispute their royalty,
May even, perchance, prevail and rule,
But never successfully.
Such, at any rate, was the stance
Of the grand, puissant pride
Over which Leo, ages since,
Had been chosen to preside.
But Leo Rex was an old-school cat
Who held as axiomatic
The firm belief that suzerains,
However aristocratic,
Have duties other and higher than
Benefiting kith.
The good of all, he dared to believe,
Was a mission, not a myth.
Of course, the good of all presupposed
Good for the leonine clan;
That was a truth so primal and firm—
Gainsay it, no one can.
But though lions deserved their privileges
They were prone to become quite greedy,
Forgetting their creed, *noblesse oblige*,
Ignoring the plight of the needy.
On the other hand, the needy were apt
To propound the most dangerous notions:
"Away with caste!" "Equality!"
And other magic potions.

The task of an elder sage was hard;
It required exquisite tact:
Appeasing the mob, reprimanding the rich—
A perilous balancing act.

*   *   *   *

One day, quite unexpectedly,
A jackal appeared on the scene,
And what ensued was the strangest sitch
Old Leo had ever seen.
The jackal was crude, ill-bred, profane—
A liar, a lout, a hack,
A popinjay, a leering roué,
A monomaniac.
To say that the beast was not their sort
Too mildly states the case,
And yet among the lion tribe
He received a warm embrace.
To their very bosoms the brute was clasped,
Into their hearts he was taken.
Why? The simple truth is this:
The beast brought home the bacon.
Through machination, deceit and chicane
The rogue had amassed great pelf
And though the avaricious brute
Never thought beyond himself
His methods, employed on a broader scale
So advantaged the elite
That in terms of material comfort and ease
Scarcely ever had life been so sweet.

They suspected, of course, that his methods were base,
But, really, all was so rosy
Prying into manner and means
Would have been inexcusably nosy.

*   *   *   *

Now here's the odd and curious thing:
The jackal not only acquired
The lion's share for the fortunate few
He made himself admired
By the many—the very animals who
The lions unfailing tried,
But never so successfully,
To keep pasi- if not satis-fied.
How he managed their wrath and discontent
To incapacitate
Was a wily trick—neither novel nor new,
But proven and potent—hate.
You see, adjoining the jungle's zone
Was a wide and vasty plain
Inhabited by creatures like
Jungle folk, in the main:
Finny, feathered, furry folk—
The guppy, the grouse, the gnu
The booby, the bat, the grizzly, the gnat,
To name there merest few.
A drought had fallen on the land
And driven its dwellers to roam
Into the jungle that *its* dwellers thought
To be their exclusive home.

The jackal defined a hungry wight
As a criminal intruder,
And his tactic worked, though his reasoning
Could hardly have been cruder
So the hate that the have-nots have for the haves
To other have-nots was deflected,
Leaving the lions to marvel at how
The switch was so neatly effected.

*   *   *   *

Now Leo was not alone in abhorring
The jackal's devious ploy.
Disgust and discontent were rife
Among the *hoi polloi*.
Not all the forest's folk, you see,
Fell for the jackal's line,
But those who didn't, every one,
Were anti-leonine;
That is to say, the very set
Which, by long tradition,
The lions had always tried to keep
In passable submission.
Old Leo observed with mounting alarm
This sad phenomenon
And did what he could to expose and scotch
The jackal's shameful con.
To no avail! Leo learned
That though being respected was nice,
The more those around him called him wise,
The more they ignored his advice.

Poor Old Leo! Late in life
He faced a doleful plight:
For once, our honest warrior saw
That the other side was right,
And publically, courageously,
He said so. But, alas,
He privately reproached himself
As a traitor to his class.
So how did it end? Old Leo died,
Sad and brokenhearted,
And the lions, hypocritically,
Mourned the dear departed.
And that's how it was that Leo's wisdom
Failed to come to his aid—
How lordly lions, goaded by greed
From the path of virtue strayed.

* * * *

Now in actual life, everyone knows
That events, once they have ended,
Are over and done, and do not come
With conclusive meanings appended.
Fables, however, end with morals,
So one may validly ask
That a fabulist face that patent fact
And undertake the task
Of declaring in no uncertain terms
The meaning of his story.
If he fails, his pointless parable
Is vain and nugatory.

Well, how about this: "Things are so bad,
One may as well give up trying,"
Or this: "No problem's so onerous
That it can't be cured by dying"?
Such lessons readers would certainly deem
To be inadmissibly dreary.
They breach the customary code:
Morals must be cheery.
So maybe this: "Things are bad,
But we're sure to find a solution,"
Or this: "No problem ever bests
Our dauntless resolution"?
Such hortatory platitudes
Are heartening and happy.
But only a fool would fail to note
That they're irredeemably sappy.
So I'll settle for this—it's neither upbeat
Nor discouragingly horrible:
"When lions play a jackal's game
The outcome is deplorable."

The Ballad of Bozo and the Bug

Mother Nature's not as kind
As she's cracked up to be,
She gives us fruit and veggies, yes,
But also this decree:

Every living thing must die,
No if's or but's about it.
You'd be a perfect idiot
If you'd try to flout it.

Still, she's cut a little slack:
She's granted us a way
Through exercise of native wit,
To delay the fatal day.

I have in mind the covid bug,
So murderous and hated,
Folks can ward that villain off
If they're vaccinated.

True, but then there's also this:
Nature isn't biased.
On a rated scale of living things,
Mankind may be highest,

But of lower, baser sorts like bugs
She also is aware.
They may lack Man's precocity,
Still they get their fair share

Of lenient consideration.
Just like Man they must,
Struggle hard to stay alive.
It's fight or bite the dust.

But although a bug's incapable
Of mental lucubration,
It's gifted with the strategy
Of hit-and-miss mutation.

It isn't rational at all,
In no wise is it shrewd,
But what the heck, it works okay
Even if it's crude.

Truth to tell, it works so well,
It give us humans fits.
Just as soon as we've devised
Some cure and call it quits

Some stupid pathogen mutates
And quite without intention
Comes up with variants that thwart
Our efforts at prevention.

Nonetheless, Man is smart
And a bug is really dense.
Reason gives a man the edge.
That's only commonsense.

He thinks things through. He knows the score.
He's wise and scientific.
He fought against the covid bug
And won—to be specific.

Well, maybe *won*'s too much to say.
So: to a draw he fought it.
Granted casualties are high
Among the folks that caught it,

But Man's innate intelligence
And rationality
Have empowered him to keep in check
The bug's brutality.

But fighting on the dumb bug's side
Is a treacherous waddahyacallum.
(I never can recall that phrase!)
Oh yes! That's it! Fifth column!

Our nation's plan to immunize
Its folk has been frustrated
By a group of rebel Bozos who
Won't be vaccinated.

Some are so dim that they refuse
A safety mask to wear.
That, they think, is tyranny,
And so they foul the air

With a spray of spit that carries with it
Covid bugs galore
That gets in other people's lungs!
I ask: could they be more

Vile and irresponsible?
If they're suicidal,
That suits me, but I object
When they turn homicidal!

(You see, I'm sure, the word I've used—
Man—upper case—
Is a vapid generality
That's seriously off base

When it's applied to living folks.
Man is just a fiction.
To deal with actuality
One need more spot-on diction.

The world is full of *men* ((of course,
That means *women* too)),
Individuals who form
A very lengthy queue:

Geniuses and flat-out dummies,
Hallowed saints and sinners,
Bosses, workers, doers, shirkers,
Experts and beginners . . . .

But why go on? My point is Man
Is brilliant and far sighted,
But taken singly, men can be
Moronic and benighted.)

Some actual men are no more sage
Or moral that my hat,
And anti-vaxxers certainly
Are instances of that.

What have the Bozos got against
A safe, life-saving shot?
You wouldn't think a person could
Give credence to such rot!

"The bug's not real. In fact it's just
A communistic trick
To shut the country down. Don't fret:
A myth can't make you sick."

Or: "Yes, the bug can make you sick,
Just keep the pest at bay
By injecting bleach into your blood
And it will go away."

Or: "Covid just pretends that it's
A terminal disease, so
Show the bully who's the boss!
The antidote's machismo.

We need to ape the plucky pose
Of our venerated chief.
Denial, swagger, virile spunk
Will bring us all relief."

So, in effect, the Bozos have
The brutal bug befriended,
But the consequences of their choice
Are strictly unintended.

They think that by ignoring it
They'll keep the bug at bay.
In fact, the bug eliminates
Folks who think this way.

The bug just does not give a damn
If the bloke it bites is bright
Or dumber that a block of wood—
Of moral wrong and right

That vicious virus does not care.
It just ain't got no smarts.
Its IQ is so low it's not
Even *on* the charts.

So, when the bug's stupidity
You seem to want to rival—
Now get this, Bozo—you imperil
Your very own survival!

My God! I simply lost my head!
Bozo won't be reading
Anything that's rational,
So what's the use of pleading?

You, dear reader, hip and savvy,
You do not require
A shaking-up. Indeed, I guess
You constitute that choir

Some preachers give their sermons to
Though it's not necessary
Because it's on the reverend's side,
Not an adversary.

Oh well, consider this, my friends:
An irony. Please savor it.
Mother Nature's bias free.
She doesn't have a favorite.

Man versus bug's a contest that,
For all that she could care,
Can turn out either way. And yet
I'd have to say she's fair.

And I suspect that secretly
She slightly favors Man,
At any rate, of Bozodom
She's clearly not a fan.

When nature's Bozos self-select
For imminent extinction
They boost Man's average IQ scores
And augment His distinction.